Essential
Time Management
and Organisation

Essential
Time Management
and Organisation

A Pocket Guide

SARAH COOK

it gp™

IT Governance Publishing

Every possible effort has been made to ensure that the information contained in this book is accurate at the time of going to press, and the publisher and the author cannot accept responsibility for any errors or omissions, however caused. No responsibility for loss or damage occasioned to any person acting, or refraining from action, as a result of the material in this publication can be accepted by the publisher or the author.

Apart from any fair dealing for the purposes of research or private study, or criticism or review, as permitted under the Copyright, Designs and Patents Act 1988, this publication may only be reproduced, stored or transmitted, in any form, or by any means, with the prior permission in writing of the publisher or, in the case of reprographic reproduction, in accordance with the terms of licences issued by the Copyright Licensing Agency. Enquiries concerning reproduction outside those terms should be sent to the publisher at the following address:

IT Governance Publishing
IT Governance Limited
Unit 3, Clive Court
Bartholomew's Walk
Cambridgeshire Business Park
Ely, Cambridgeshire
CB7 4EH
United Kingdom

www.itgovernance.co.uk

First published in the United Kingdom in 2011
by IT Governance Publishing.

ISBN: 978-1-84928-302-1

PREFACE

In today's business environment, there is increasing pressure on managers to do more with less. Technology has empowered people in the working environment, yet it has also increased expectations of speed of response and delivery. There is increasing pressure, therefore, for people to be more organised, and to plan and use their time effectively.

The book is a practical tool intended to help you develop your time management and organisational skills. It outlines the principles of effective time management and discusses how business professionals can develop these skills. It provides tools and techniques as well as self-assessment questionnaires and exercises that you can use to enhance your effectiveness at work.

Essential time management and organisation requires discipline and determination. By applying the techniques in this book, I am sure you will achieve greater performance at work.

Sarah Cook

Managing Director
The Stairway Consultancy Ltd.

www.thestairway.co.uk

ABOUT THE AUTHOR

Sarah Cook is the Managing Director of The Stairway Consultancy Ltd. She has over 20 years' consulting experience, specialising in leadership and management development. Prior to this, Sarah worked for Unilever and as the Head of Customer Care for a retail marketing consultancy.

Sarah has practical experience of helping managers to improve the way they manage and organise their time. She has written widely on the topics of time management, leadership, management development, team building and coaching. She also speaks regularly on these subjects at conferences and seminars.

Sarah is a Fellow of the Chartered Institute of Personnel and Development and is a Chartered Marketer. She has an MA from Cambridge University and an MBA, and is an accredited user of a wide range of psychometric and team diagnostic tools.

For more information about The Stairway Consultancy, please see *www.thestairway.co.uk* or contact *sarah@thestairway.co.uk*.

ACKNOWLEDGEMENTS

The contents of this book are based on my own experience from the work I have done with a wide range of managers and IT professionals to help improve their time management and organisational skills.

We are grateful to the two reviewers of this book for their helpful insights: ir H.L. (Maarten) Souw RE IT Auditor, UWV and Trevor Wood, Director, Redline Digital Services Ltd.

CONTENTS

Contents

CHAPTER 1: HOW SUCCESSFUL ARE YOU AS A TIME MANAGER?

One thing that is immutable in this world is the number of hours we have in a day. The challenge for the business professional is to make the best use of the time that they spend at work, so that they are both efficient (doing things right) and effective (doing the right things).

I am sure we all go to work with good intentions, but many of us fail to achieve the key tasks of the day. Distractions, competing priorities and the sheer volume of work can all mean that projects slip, objectives and KPIs are not met and stress levels rise within the workplace.

So how do you ensure that you achieve your workload? How do you put in place a system to ensure better organisation and achievement of tasks?

Recognise where you are now

The first step in any improvement action is to recognise how effective you currently are as a time manager. How well organised are you?

Here is a simple self-assessment checklist that can help you do this. Score a 'Yes' if you generally do the following and a 'No' if you generally do not. Be honest with yourself!

No.	Questions	Yes	No
1.	When you arrive in the office in the morning, do you have a written plan (made out the day before) as to how you will spend most of your day at work?		

2.	Do you give priority to the things that must be done, rather than the things you like to do?		
3.	Do you know what time of day you work most effectively and, therefore, use this time for working on your most difficult tasks?		
4.	Do you keep your desk clear of all papers except those on which you are working?		
5.	Do you have an effective system for dealing with your e-mails?		
6.	Do you end up doing tasks that you could potentially delegate to others?		
7.	Do you have a tendency to take on more that you can realistically achieve?		
8.	Do you 'butterfly' from one task to another?		
9.	Are you harassed by frequent interruptions that affect your ability to		

	concentrate?		
10.	Do you frequently put off an assignment until it becomes an emergency or panic situation?		

Your score

To see how good you are at time management and organisation, look back at your answers.

For questions 1 to 5, award yourself 10 points for each 'Yes' and 1 point for each 'No'.

For questions 6 to 10, award yourself 10 points for each 'No' and 1 point for each 'Yes'.

Then total your scores.

Score 75–100: You are a good time manager.

You are an extremely well-organised professional who knows that good working habits save time and reduce stress.

Score 40–74: Your time management could be improved.

The way you organise your work may sometimes create problems for yourself and others. Greater time management and self-discipline would help you achieve more at work.

Score 39 or less: You are a poor time manager.

You are wasting an awful lot of time by failing to organise yourself and your work. As a result, you are probably not achieving your objectives and may feel that you are working under undue pressure and stress.

Improving your time management and organisation

The following diagram outlines the process that you can adopt to make improvements in how effective and efficient you are at work:

Figure 1: The time management process

Effective time management involves three key steps:

1. Establishing responsibilities, priorities and objectives.
2. Eliminating unnecessary and inappropriate activities.
3. Planning and scheduling the use of your time on a daily and monthly basis.

The chapters in this book will provide you with handy tips and advice to improve your time management and organisation, based on these three principles.

Your motivation to improve your time management

If you really want to improve the way you manage your time, you must be willing to change the way you work. Poor time management is invariably the result of bad habits. You won't get anywhere unless you admit this to yourself. The reality is that habits are easier to make than they are to break. If you repeat a behaviour often enough, it becomes a habit. There is an old saying: 'Bad habits are like a comfortable bed – easy to get into, but hard to get out of'.

If you are a poor time manager, you need to replace poor habits with better ones. Select an aspect of your time management that you feel motivated to change, and focus on this. It is reckoned that it takes at least a month to form new habits, so, in applying the techniques in this book, you will need to be determined and persevere.

Visualise the new, organised you. See it, hear it, feel it. Hear the compliments you will receive when you get things done. Feel how great it is to make this change.

You may find it useful to discuss with someone the changes you are going to make in the way you manage your time. This could be with a colleague, coach or close friend. Use them to help you review progress, to celebrate success and to keep you focused on your time management improvement goal.

CHAPTER 2: SETTING OBJECTIVES, GOALS AND PRIORITIES

Establishing goals

I imagine that you may have a goal in mind in reading this book: perhaps to improve your time management and effectiveness? At work, whatever our responsibilities, we have goals, objectives and targets that we have to meet. The place to start when improving your time management is to be clear about your key performance indicators. These are the criteria by which your performance will be measured. They outline what you have to achieve, how to achieve it and by when.

This chapter will help you clarify your goals and objectives. In it, I will also introduce a practical process for prioritising the tasks you have to achieve to meet your objectives.

Be a macro- not a micromanager

One of the symptoms of poor time management is being trapped in a cycle of having too much to do. The result is that we tend to micromanage tasks, often applying a scatter-gun approach and spreading ourselves too thinly. In order to be effective time managers, we need to be able to stand back, take a helicopter view and focus on the macro goals we are working towards.

Set SMART objectives

In order to be an effective time manager, you need to be clear about what you need to achieve and by when. You may find it helpful to do this on a monthly basis, before focusing on what you need to achieve each week and each day.

Take a moment to consider and make a list of the goals you need to accomplish in the next month. Make sure that these are SMART – **S**pecific, **M**easurable, **A**chievable, **R**ealistic and **T**ime-bound. For example:

- To have completed Phase 1 of the software installation project by the end of the month.
- To have undertaken a project implementation review for the integration project by 20th of the month.
- To have held appraisals for all staff by the end of the month.
- To have organised a team away day by the end of the month.

If your list is very long, ask yourself:

- What are the key goals, the 'must achieves' this month, rather than the 'nice to achieves'?
- What are the key performance indicators that need to be accomplished?
- Does everything on your list have to be achieved this month?

It is far better to have three to six key goals that you can achieve in the month than 20 that you are unlikely to accomplish.

Having established your goals for the month, now turn your attention to the tasks you need to accomplish in order to achieve your goals. You will probably end up with a long list of tasks that you need to do, but which are your top priorities?

Prioritising tasks

To establish priorities, you need consider two elements:

- The URGENCY of the task in relation to TIME, e.g. when does the task need to be achieved?
- The IMPORTANCE of the task in relation to the ORGANISATIONAL NEED, e.g. is the task related to one of your key objectives?

Having listed your tasks, use the following ranking system to set the order of priority:

A = Urgent and important tasks – these need to be completed within a short deadline and are vital to the achievement of your objectives.

B = Important, but not urgent, tasks – tasks which are vital to the achievement of your objectives, but where you have a longer time to achieve them.

C = Not important, but urgent, tasks – activities which need to be completed in a short time span, but which are not vital to the achievement of organisational objectives.

D = Not important and not urgent tasks. These are activities which are not critical to the achievement of your objectives and for which time is not of the essence.

This system can be represented graphically as follows:

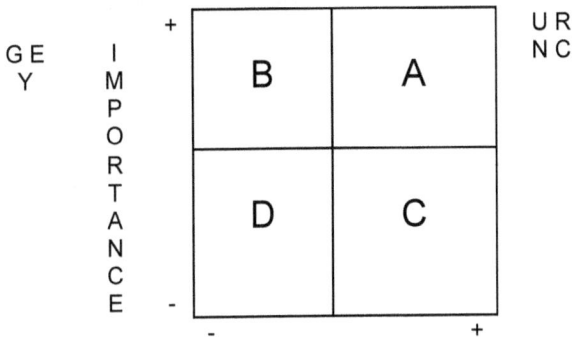

Figure 2: The priority ranking system

Using the priority ranking system

If, after prioritising your list, you have a number of tasks in each category, allocate an order of priority to each of the As, Bs, Cs and Ds – e.g. A1, A2, A3, A4, etc.

The temptation is to start working on C tasks – the not important, but urgent, ones. However, the best time managers work through all the As, then the Bs and then the Cs. This means that they concentrate on the few critical tasks, rather than the too many less important ones.

Why start the B tasks – the important but not urgent tasks – before the C tasks? The danger with important tasks that are not required to be completed immediately is that you delay them until they become A tasks – both important and urgent. By planning and tackling important activities before their deadlines, you will avoid last-minute pressures and stress.

Ds are tasks that are not important or urgent, so you can either dump them or, if appropriate, delegate them. Certainly, these should not be the focus of your energies.

When new tasks appear, slot them into your ranking system.

Remember to review your list of tasks, using the ranking system, on a regular basis, to ensure that you focus on your key priorities.

CHAPTER 3: PLANNING YOUR TIME

Having set and/or clarified your objectives and key priorities, you can now plan your time. In this chapter, we will look at typical problems that arise when planning activities and how to overcome them.

Are you a procrastinator?

Some people like to plan and be organised; others tend to let things happen as they come along, and are unplanned and unstructured. In order to be an effective time manager, you need to create a plan and stick to it.

Do you focus only on today?

A common problem when planning is the temptation to look more widely at what needs to be achieved in the week, or the month, or the year, rather than only to consider the tasks for the day ahead.

The monthly, weekly and daily planner (see below) will help you overcome this.

Do you underestimate the time you lose each day and overestimate the time you have to complete tasks?

Given that most people's working day is eight hours, when you take off time for lunch and breaks and this amounts to roughly six and a half hours (assuming that you do take lunch and breaks – more of this later!). It is estimated that at least a third of the working day is taken up with interruptions and unexpected events, so, in reality, the time you have in the day to complete your tasks is approximately four hours. This presupposes you have nothing else in your diary.

The OATS process is a useful system for clarifying exactly what needs to be done, when it needs to be done and how much time you actually have in which to do it.

The OATS process

One way in which you can plan your time effectively is to adopt the OATS process at the beginning of each month, each week and each day. This involves:

O = Objectives. As described in the previous chapter, make a list of what you need to accomplish this month/week/day.

A = Activities. Create a list of what you have to do in order to achieve your objectives.

T = Time. Consider realistically how much time it will take to perform these activities. Then consider how much time you actually have.

S = Schedule. Use a planner or a calendar to place each of the activities in a priority sequence. Focus on achieving the important tasks rather than just on the things you enjoy doing.

The act of writing down your objectives and activities for the month allows you to put them into a sequence, taking into consideration the other events that you have in your calendar.

Rather than having long lists of things to do, it is important to focus each month, week and day on your key priorities. I recommend that you restrict your work plan to up to five key activities you need to achieve each day, week or month.

People tend to underestimate how long it will take to carry out an activity. Be realistic about how long each task is likely to take. Set yourself a starting time for each activity, as well as a target finishing time to complete the tasks associated with each objective.

I recommend that you use a planning schedule. Here is one that I find helpful. There are three versions of this schedule that you can adapt for your own use: monthly, weekly and daily. This can be linked to your e-mail application's calendar, so that you can diarise tasks.

Monthly schedule

List your key objectives for the month:

1. _____
2. _____
3. _____
4. _____
5. _____

List the key tasks you need to carry out in order to achieve your objectives. Then, taking into consideration your other commitments over the month, plan when you will start and finish these activities.

Week	Key activities
1	
2	
3	
4	

Weekly schedule

Create a weekly schedule with reference to the objectives you need to achieve over the month.

List your key objectives for the week:

1. _____
2. _____
3. _____
4. _____

5. _____

List the key tasks you need to carry out in order to achieve your objectives. Next, taking your other commitments into consideration, plan when during the week you will start and finish these activities.

Remember to schedule the most important tasks, so that you do these at the beginning of the week, rather than leaving them to the end.

Week	Key activities
Monday	
Tuesday	
Wednesday	
Thursday	
Friday	

Daily schedule

When creating a daily 'to do' list, group together related work. So, for example, it is quicker and more efficient to reply to your e-mails in batches at specific times during the day than to interrupt other tasks to read e-mails and reply sporadically.

It is tempting to focus on the tasks we like most, rather than on those we enjoy less but which need to be done. So remember to schedule in the tasks that are most important or difficult at your peak energy time. (See Chapter 4 to find out when this is, if you are not sure.)

Schedule yesterday's uncompleted tasks into today's programme, and do them first.

If you have major tasks to achieve, break these down into manageable chunks. You will feel more satisfaction in achieving these smaller activities and the overall task will be less daunting.

List your key objectives for the day:

1. _____

2. _____

3. _____

4. _____

5. _____

Then plan your day:

Time	Priority (A, B or C)	Activity
9.00–9.30		
9.30–10.00		
10.00–10.30		

and so on.

To summarise, in order to plan your time effectively:

1. Be clear about your goals for each month, each week and each day.
2. Plan ahead – put planning time as a task in your diary.

3. Set time aside at the end of each month to plan for the following month, at the end of each week to plan for the following week and at the end of each day for the following day.

4. As soon as you know you have a project, a meeting or a presentation coming up, plan time in your diary to prepare for this. Block out 'preparation time' and arrange for your colleagues to cover for you.

5. Allocate yourself deadlines to begin tasks, as well as deadlines to complete them.

CHAPTER 4: AVOIDING TIMEWASTERS

There may be aspects of your daily life where you are wasting, not saving, time. In this chapter, we will look at how you can make use of your peak energy time, how to analyse where you are spending your time, how to identify timewasters and take action to overcome these.

Are you a morning or an evening person?

Before identifying what is wasting your time, it is useful to analyse when during the day you are at your best – when you have the most energy and, therefore, when you are likely to achieve more.

By answering the following questions, you can find out whether you are a morning or an evening type of person. This will help you plan your day, so that you undertake the most difficult, important or urgent work during this time. It will also help you identify when, in particular, you need uninterrupted time without distractions and timewasters.

Look at the questionnaire below and assume it is a normal working day. Answer the questions as honestly as possible.

1. At what time do you go to bed at night?

(a)	after 1 am	Score 3
(b)	between 11.30 pm and 1 am	Score 2
(c)	between 10 pm and 11.30 pm	Score 1
(d)	before 10 pm	Score 0

2. Do you have difficulty getting out of bed when you wake up in the mornings?

(a)	very often	Score 3
(b)	sometimes	Score 2
(c)	seldom	Score 1
(d)	very seldom	Score 0

3. During the first hour after waking in the morning which would you prefer?

(a) full breakfast   Score 0
(b) continental breakfast   Score 1
(c) boiled egg   Score 2
(d) tea, coffee or herbal drink   Score 3

4. When you do have commitments early the next day, how early do you go to bed compared with a normal day?

(a) more than two hours earlier   Score 0
(b) one to two hours earlier   Score 1
(c) up to one hour earlier   Score 2
(d) no earlier   Score 3

5. Think back to times when you have had disagreements with your colleagues at work or felt 'out of sorts', even if you didn't express it. Were these times:

(a) mainly before lunch?   Score 3
(b) mainly after lunch?   Score 1

6. Use the timer on your phone or look at your watch or a clock with a second hand, then look away and estimate the passage of one minute without any help. Then check your estimate. Was this:

(a) under 1 minute?   Score 1
(b exactly 1 minute?   Score 2
(b) over 1 minute ?   Score 3

Now total your scores.

The lower your score, the more of a morning type you are. So if you scored between 6 and 9 points, you are likely to work best in the mornings and, ideally, should use the time before lunch to do your 'A' tasks. If your score is higher (10 and above), you are more of an evening type, so use the afternoons onwards to carry out your critical tasks.

Energy flows

To verify your peak energy time, take a typical working day and plot the ebb and flow of your energy throughout the day. Mark on the chart when you eat and when you take a break, as these can have a direct effect on your energy.

Typically, when people have lots to do, they become glued to their desks. Yet, research shows that movement provides more oxygen to the brain. Our attention span also diminishes after 20 minutes of undertaking the same task. Make a point of taking breaks, getting a breath of fresh air and eating on a regular basis. Get up from your desk, even if it is just for a stretch every 20–30 minutes. There are many software programmes that remind you to do this, if this is a habit you think might be beneficial to you.

Identifying timewasters

Having analysed at what time of the day you work best and how to increase your energy levels, let's look now at how you can save time by eliminating timewasters.

A proven way of doing this is to analyse how you spend your time in a typical working week. You can use an online calendar to record what you do every half-hour. Look back over the week, and then list timewasters and their probable causes.

Next, identify strategies that will help you avoid, or minimise, the things that waste your time. Set yourself an objective to eliminate the inconsequential things that steal most of your time.

Identify your own timewasters

Assess which activities waste your time by answering the following questions.

Score a 'Yes' if you generally do the following and a 'No' if you generally do not.

No.	Questions	Yes	No
1.	Do you find yourself attending too many meetings?		
2.	Do you find it hard to concentrate, shifting from one task to another?		
3.	Do you take on too much work?		
4.	Are you plagued by interruptions?		
5.	Do you look at the Internet and social media sites during work time?		
6.	Do you enjoy chatting to colleagues when you should be working?		
7.	Do you find yourself interrupting others' work?		
8.	Do the meetings you hold run to time?		

If you have answered 'Yes' for questions 1 to 5, you could well be wasting your time. Refer to tips 1 to 5 in the 'Strategies to overcome timewasters' section below.

If you have answered 'Yes' to questions 6 to 8, you potentially are wasting other people's time as well as your own! Consider how your actions may be impacting others. For example, it is good to chat, but for how long do you do this? Can you wait to speak to other people at a set time, rather than interrupting them on a frequent basis? Can you improve your meeting management skills?

Strategies to overcome timewasters

Here is a list of potential timewasters, linked to the questionnaire you have just completed. Pay particular attention to the ones that apply to you, and select actions you can take to overcome these.

1. Too many meetings

- Ask yourself:
  - o Do you have to go to them all?
  - o Do you have to be present for the entire meeting or could you attend or dial in for just part of it?
  - o Could someone else go in your place?
  - o Do the meetings need to be held on such a regular basis?
  - o Can you make the meeting shorter? (If you set aside an hour for a meeting, invariably it will last an hour. Table the meeting for 40 minutes and see what happens!)

- Put up a clock where everyone can see it.

- Have an agenda with time slots allocated to all the items.

2. Time wasted shifting from one task to another

- Work on one item at a time.

- Keep your in-tray away from your desk – you won't be tempted to shuffle its contents.

- Have a tidy desk.

- Organise your e-mails (see the next chapter) and only look at and reply to them at one scheduled time during the day.

- Handle each piece of paper only once.

- Set yourself a target time to complete a task. When you have accomplished it, give yourself a break or a 'reward'.

3. Taking on too much work

- Delegate/share the workload.

- Say 'No' to jobs that aren't yours.

4. Interruptions

- Put your phone on voicemail, or ask a colleague to answer it for you so you have uninterrupted time to plan and to carry out important and urgent tasks.

- Find a meeting room, or a quiet space, to complete important tasks without interruption.

- Be assertive – ask the person who interrupts you to come back later.

- Stand up or perch on the edge of the desk when someone comes to see you. This signals to them that you do not have much time.

- Ask the person to prepare a list of points to raise with you and look at them together in one go. This should avoid them needing to interrupt you constantly.

- Spend five minutes in the morning planning the day with your team.

- If you are interrupted, write down where you have got to with the task in hand. It makes it easier to come back to it.

5. Surfing the Net

- Logging on to the Internet or Facebook may be tempting, but invariably one always spends longer than anticipated surfing the Net.
- Ask yourself whether this is an essential part of your work? Can you undertake this activity elsewhere? Can you set yourself a time limit for how long you will devote to this activity? Is it really a priority?

CHAPTER 5: E-MAIL MANAGEMENT

A vast proportion of work activity is now centred around e-mails. Although they are a powerful business tool, unless you control and manage them, response times can slip, and critical actions and deadlines will be missed. In this chapter, we will look at a useful approach to managing your e-mails. The principles apply to whatever e-mail application you use.

Don't be an e-mail junkie

Do you look at your e-mails and reply to them throughout the day? Are you a slave to instant messaging and/or the alerts that notify you every time you receive an e-mail?

I appreciate that it is important to scan e-mails during the day to pick up urgent messages or requests. However, by looking at and replying to or actioning e-mails constantly throughout the day, you interrupt the flow of your work and become less efficient.

Likewise, if you leave your e-mails to pile up, you can become overwhelmed by the number of them and feel reluctant to take any action. It is estimated that, on average, people receive between 60 and 100 e-mails per day, so if you leave them for a while, or if you are out of the office, they can quickly pile up.

Best practice is to schedule uninterrupted time each day to manage your e-mails. Make a regular appointment in your calendar to do this, and make sure you won't be interrupted. Get into the habit of dealing with all your e-mails during this time.

Organise your e-mail folders

In order to take control of your e-mails, it is essential to have a method of organising your e-mail folders. This will give you a structure to work to. Take some time to explore the functionality of your e-mail application. It is surprising how much can be done to manage e-mails simply by gaining a greater understanding of what your e-mail application can do for you.

It is estimated that up to a third of e-mails are for reference only, so you may wish to distinguish these e-mails from those you need to action. Look at whether you are the key recipient of the e-mail, or whether you have been copied into it; this should give you a good indication of whether any action is required, or if the e-mail is just for your reference. Whatever e-mail application you use, you will find details of how to set up a reference system in the Help function of your application.

You may wish to consider having folders, or subfolders, for each project, or topic, and to separate out the e-mails where you need to take action and those that are for reference. You can use your calendar, or task list, to remind you to complete the actions, and to show you when they have been completed.

Working through your e-mails

As tempting as it may seem to jump from one e-mail to another, this wastes, rather than saves, time. If there are a lot of e-mails in your inbox, the best strategy, unless you know that some are particularly urgent, is to work through them one by one in date order.

There will be e-mails in your inbox that are more important than others. Most applications allow you to filter by date, by subject, by conversation groups, or by the sender or receiver of the e-mail message. The reading or preview pane will also allow you to view messages without having to open them.

The 4D model for dealing with e-mails

Once you have opened an e-mail, aim in three out of four cases to handle the message only once. This saves time and increases your efficiency. The 4D model gives you four decision options:

- **Do** it

- **D**iarise it
- **D**elegate it
- **D**elete it.

Do it

When you open an e-mail and it calls for an action, aim to do it there and then. You will find that 80% of e-mails can be actioned in less than five minutes. This might involve replying, making a phone call or simply filing the e-mail. By actioning the e-mail there and then you save time and increase efficiency.

Diarise it

You will probably find that there will be about 20% of e-mails that you cannot action within five minutes. In these cases, add them to the 'to do' list in your diary and allocate a priority to each e-mail. You can put the action in your calendar, or use your application's task list as a reminder.

Delegate it

There may be some actions that you can delegate or need to share with others. In these cases, forward the e-mail after you have read it: send a covering e-mail then send it on there and then. Move the original e-mail to your filing reference system.

Delete it

When you read an e-mail, ask yourself:

- Do you need to action this?
- Do you need it for reference?
- Do other people need to know or action the e-mail?

If the answer to all these questions is 'No', delete the mail. Be disciplined in this respect – effectively these are items that are not urgent or important, so why keep them?

By following the 4D model every day, you can deal with the majority of e-mails within an hour or so and improve your efficiency and effectiveness.

CHAPTER 6: DELEGATION TECHNIQUES

When it comes to becoming a better time manager, the ability to delegate is a fundamental skill. Delegation will help you achieve tasks by sharing decision making and authority, whilst retaining the ultimate accountability for a task. In this chapter, we will consider why some people are reluctant to delegate, and I will provide some tips on how to delegate effectively.

Why do people not delegate?

Whilst I advocate that you concentrate personally on those tasks whose success depends on you, it is a proven fact that a greater number of tasks can be achieved by a number of people, rather than relying on a few. Learning to delegate will help you become both a better time manager and a better people manager. So why are people reluctant to delegate?

Sometimes I have heard people say that they have no one to delegate to. However, people do not work in isolation, and everyone has colleagues and team members. If someone has a particularly onerous workload, it is possible to enlist support from colleagues and team members via their manager. It is also possible to delegate upwards!

So what is the major blockage to delegation? I believe it is primarily one of fear:

- Fear of losing work allocated to you, if you delegate tasks and they are done well.
- Fear that your subordinate, or colleague, won't do the job to your required standards, or in the requisite time.
- Fear that the other person cannot be trusted to do the job
- Fear that the other person will make a mistake, and that you will have to carry the responsibility for not completing the task.

To be able to delegate implies recognition that others can help you do a better job than you can do alone, in terms of not only quantity but also quality. If you have a backlog of unfinished work, or realise that something needs to be done to help you be more effective and get things done, then delegation is the way forward.

Tips on how to delegate

It is important to recognise what needs to happen in the stages of delegation – before, during and after. If you give too many directives and check up too much, the assignee will feel that they are not trusted and are really considered incapable of acting on their own initiative.

Before delegating the task

Plan what you will delegate and to whom. Consider whether to delegate whole tasks, or parts, to grow the individual's competence and confidence. Select the person to do the task, and consider what support they will need to do it. If the person is new to the task, accept a reasonable number of beginner's mistakes without irritation and help them to find their feet.

During

Make sure you explain fully to the person to whom you are delegating what they have to do and why the job has to be done. This means they will appreciate the importance of the job and feel that what they are doing is worthwhile. Set parameters – what results do you require and by when, and to what standards. Most importantly, if you are delegating authority, too, tell the person what authority they have to do the job. Inform others with whom they may come into contact, or need to deal, about this, too.

As the job progresses, it is appropriate to carry out checks at agreed points and offer help, if it is needed. Do this, ideally, with a degree of informality, so that the person does not feel they are being overly checked up on. Encourage the person to let you know what is happening and, at the same time, offer both motivational and developmental feedback.

After

On completion of the task, ensure you review the job and provide feedback. Give praise for things well done and offer suggestions about what could be done differently or better. Use the experience as a training exercise, if the opportunity offers itself, with pointers to drive better performance in future.

By adopting these principles, you will not only develop better time management practices, but also help to grow and develop other people.

CHAPTER 7: SUMMARY AND OVERVIEW OF TIME MANAGEMENT TOOLS AND TECHNIQUES

In this short guide, I have provided tools and techniques to improve your time management skills. By way of a summary, this chapter gives you the opportunity to review some of the principle techniques in this book and to identify key areas where you wish to improve.

Good time management ideas

The ideas on the following pages will help you to become a better time manager. In order to achieve this, read all the tips and then select the two that you believe are the most important in helping you become better organised. This may not seem very many, but the reason I recommend that you take on board two out of the 34 ideas is that you are more likely to implement these than if you set yourself an unachievable target.

I suggest that you highlight the two ideas you select and put them into action straightaway.

Prioritising

1. Be clear about your objectives for the month, the week and the day.
2. Arrange and allocate your priorities for each task. Use the categorisations A, B, C and D.
3. Throw away the Ds. These are tasks that are neither urgent nor important.
4. Subdivide your As into A1, A2, A3, etc.
5. Do task A1 first, followed by your other A tasks – not those attractive Cs!

Planning

6. Make appointments with yourself in your diary for planning.

7. Plan at the end of each day for the following day and at the end of each week for the following week.
8. Chop a big task down into smaller, more manageable pieces.
9. Estimate the end time for a task, not just the start time.
10. When planning, allow time for unexpected events.
11. Make sure you complete a monthly plan, as well as a weekly and a daily plan.
12. Don't include too many items on your list of things to do.
13. Maintain a second 'to do' list for longer-term tasks or those to which a date cannot yet be given.
14. Record what you have to do – don't try to keep your 'to do' lists in your head.

Avoiding timewasters

15. Analyse how you spend your time.
16. Identify your biggest timewasters and address these.
17. Be assertive: learn to say 'No'.
18. Recognise your peak energy time, and use this to achieve your most important and urgent, or difficult, tasks.
19. If interrupted during a task, write down your next thoughts; when you return to your task, you will know what you were going to do next.

E-mail management

20. Respond to e-mails (unless urgent) at a diarised time each day.
21. Use the 4D process for e-mails – Do it, Diarise it, Delegate it, Delete it.
22. Become familiar with the functionality of your e-mail application and what is available to help you organise your e-mails.
23. Turn off your incoming e-mail notification alert.
24. Aim to handle 80% of e-mails only once, if at all possible.

Delegating

25. Delegate whenever possible: downwards, sideways or upwards.
26. Delegate tasks, but do not abdicate them: if it is your task, you still have the final responsibility.
27. Always make the instructions for the tasks you delegate complete and clear, and ensure that they have been understood.
28. Always give, or agree, a completion date for the delegated task.
29. Agree the reviews which will be part of the delegation process.
30. Allow people to whom you have delegated the freedom to complete the task. Don't interrupt at times when you haven't agreed to do so.

Discipline

31. Do the unpleasant task first.
32. Stick to the task you know must be done.
33. Do one thing at a time.
34. Get everyone else in your team to think about effective time management.

Self-discipline and time management

There is a saying: 'Unless you change how you are, you will always have what you've got'. Ultimately, effective time management and organisation is all about self-discipline. I wish you the motivation and the self-determination to master the techniques in this book in order to become a better time manager.

Good luck!

Sarah Cook
The Stairway Consultancy Ltd.

7: Summary and overview of time management tools and techniques

www.thestairway.co.uk

EU for product safety is Stephen Evans, The Mill Enterprise Hub, Stagreenan, Drogheda, Co. Louth, A92 CD3D, Ireland. (servicecentre@itgovernance.eu)

www.ingramcontent.com/pod-product-compliance
Lightning Source LLC
Chambersburg PA
CBHW070920210326
41521CB00010B/2258